Welcome to Kenya

By Patrick Ryan

The Child's World®

Published by The Child's World®
1980 Lookout Drive
Mankato, MN 56003-1705
800-599-READ
www.childsworld.com

Content Adviser: Professor Gichana C. Manyara,
Department of Geography, Radford University, Radford, VA
Design and Production: The Creative Spark, San Juan Capistrano, CA
Editorial: Emily J. Dolbear, Brookline, MA
Photo Research: Deborah Goodsite, Califon, NJ

Cover and title page: Tom Cockrem/Lonely Planet Images
Interior photos: Alamy: 9 bottom (David Keith Jones/Images of Africa Photobank), 16 (Travelshots.com),
18 (Marion Kaplan), 29 (LMR Group), 30 (Jenny Matthews); AP Photo: 7 (Karel Prinsloo), 25 (Jason
DeCrow); Corbis: 6 (Sally A. Morgan; Ecoscene), 14 (Wendy Stone), 17 (Roger De La Harpe; Gallo Images),
20 (Paul Souders); Getty Images: 12 (Central Press); iStockphoto.com: 28 (Ufuk Zivana), 31 (Robert
Hardholt); Landov: 13, 27 (Xinhua); John Warburton-Lee Photography: 9 top (John Warburton-Lee), 3, 10
(Nigel Pavitt); Lonely Planet Images: 22 (Eric Wheater); Minden Pictures: 3, 8 (Thomas Mangelsen); NASA
Earth Observatory: 4 (Reto Stockli); Oxford Scientific: 15 (Ron Johnson/Index Stock Imagery), 19 (Liba
Taylor/Robert Harding Picture Library Ltd); Panos Pictures: 21 (Betty Press), 23 (Trygve Bolstad), 3, 24
(Crispin Hughes).
Map: XNR Productions: 5

Library of Congress Cataloging-in-Publication Data
Ryan, Patrick, 1948–
  Welcome to Kenya / by Patrick Ryan.
      p. cm. — (Welcome to the world)
  Includes index.
  ISBN-13: 978-1-59296-919-7 (library bound : alk. paper)
  ISBN-10: 1-59296-919-4 (library bound : alk. paper)
  1. Kenya—Juvenile literature. I. Title.

DT433.522.R935 2007
967.62—dc22
                                            2007005559

Contents

Where Is Kenya?

From outer space, Earth looks blue. That's the color of the oceans. These deep seas surround many darker land areas called continents. Some continents are made up of many different countries. Some countries are large, and some are small. Kenya is a large country on the continent of Africa.

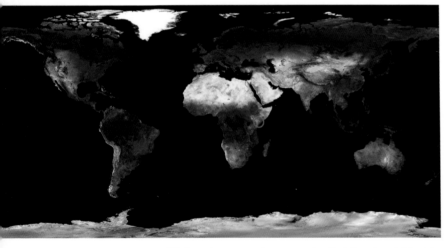

This picture gives us a flat look at Earth.
Kenya is inside the red circle.

Did you know?

The **equator** is an imaginary line around the middle of the earth. It divides Kenya almost in half.

SUDAN

Ilemi Triangle

ETHIOPIA

0   50   100 miles
0   50   100 kilometers

Lodwar •

Lake Turkana

Marsabit •

UGANDA

Wajir •

SOMALIA

Eldoret •

Kisumu •

Meru •

Nakuru •

Garissa •

Lake Victoria

Thika •

Nairobi ⊛

Machakos •

INDIAN OCEAN

KENYA

⊛ National capital

• Other city

--- Disputed border

Malindi •

Mombasa •

TANZANIA

N
W ⊗ E
S

Animals drink at a watering hole near mountains in Kilaguni.

The Land

Kenya is a country of many landscapes. There are many mountains. There are miles of sunny beaches. Most of all, there are wide, grassy plains. These huge grasslands are called **savannas**. Many animals run free on Kenya's savannas.

Kenya also has rich farmland. In some areas, warm weather and lots of rainfall help many types of plants to grow. Some of these areas are covered with tea and coffee fields that farmers plant each year.

Did you **know?**

Kenya is named after its highest point—Mount Kenya, 17,057 feet (5,199 meters) high. Mount Kenya (above) is the second-highest mountain in Africa.

A female leopard rests in the grass at Kenya's Masai Mara National Reserve.

Plants and Animals

In some parts of Kenya, people don't have to go to the zoo
to see wild animals, they just go to the country! Elephants,
cheetahs, leopards, and lions all roam Kenya's grassy plains.

Giraffes, ostriches, antelope, and zebras live there, too. Many of the animals graze on the grasses that grow on the savannas.

But there are also many other kinds of plants there. One cactus plant in Kenya looks like a bunch of candlesticks. Another strange plant is the baobab (BOW-bab) tree. It is not

Did you **know?**

Kenya is the land of the **safari**. A safari (above) is a trip on the savanna to see wild animals. Each year, thousands of people go on safaris in Kenya's many national parks and wildlife **reserves**.

tall, but it has a fat trunk. The tree stores water inside its thick trunk to use during dry weather.

A baobab tree with green leaves in the rainy season

9

A view of Kenya's Great Rift Valley

Long Ago

Thousands of years ago, earthquakes and volcanoes made a deep valley in the earth's surface. Part of this huge area, called the Great Rift Valley, runs right through Kenya. Scientists think that the Great Rift Valley is where the first relatives of all of the earth's people lived.

Much later, wandering people began to travel to Kenya. Some of these people settled down and built houses and villages. Others lived on the open savanna, raising herds of cows and goats. Over time, more people came to Kenya. They formed different **ethnic groups**. Each group had its own language and way of life.

Years later, more newcomers, or **immigrants**, came to Kenya from places such as Europe. They were looking for good land to farm and places to raise their animals. Sometimes the immigrants would take the land of the local ethnic groups and force them to work on it.

11

Kenya Today

At one time, the country of Great Britain ruled Kenya. But today, Kenyans have freedom. They have their own

government and president. And much of the land that was taken away from the local ethnic groups has been given back. A Kenyan named Jomo Kenyatta led the country to independence in 1963. He became Kenya's first prime minister and later the country's first president.

President Jomo Kenyatta in 1965

12

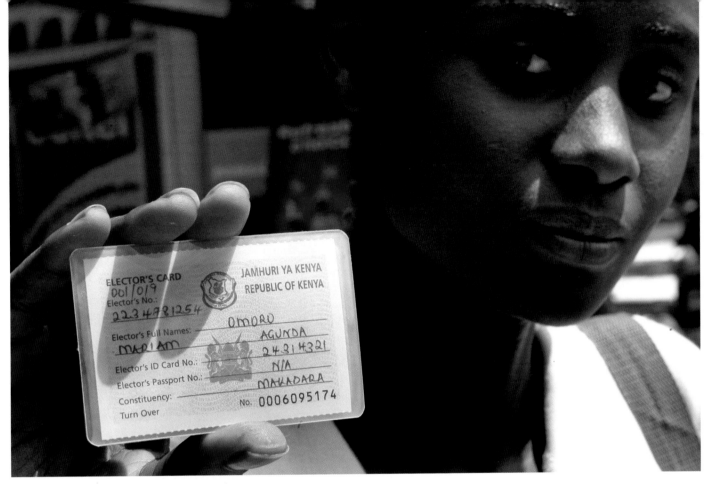

A Kenyan proudly shows her voter identification card in 2006.

During difficult times, Kenyans have learned that working together is the only real way to solve problems. They try hard each day to make their country a better place to live.

13

The People

Kenya has more than 40 different ethnic groups. They include the Kikuyu (kee-KOO-yoo), the Luhya, the Luo (loo-OH), the Kalenjin, the Kamba, the Kisii, and the Masai (mah-SIGH) people. Just as they did long ago, each group has its own ideas and ways of life.

They often sing, dance, and tell stories to remember the ways of long ago. A few Kenyans still live as their relatives did hundreds of years ago. In Kenya, remembering the ways of the past is important.

Did you **know?**

A Kikuyu college professor named Wangari Maathai (above) won the Nobel Peace Prize in 2004. Maathai founded an organization, called the Green Belt Movement, that paid women to plant trees in Kenya's shrinking forests. She was the first African woman to receive the award.

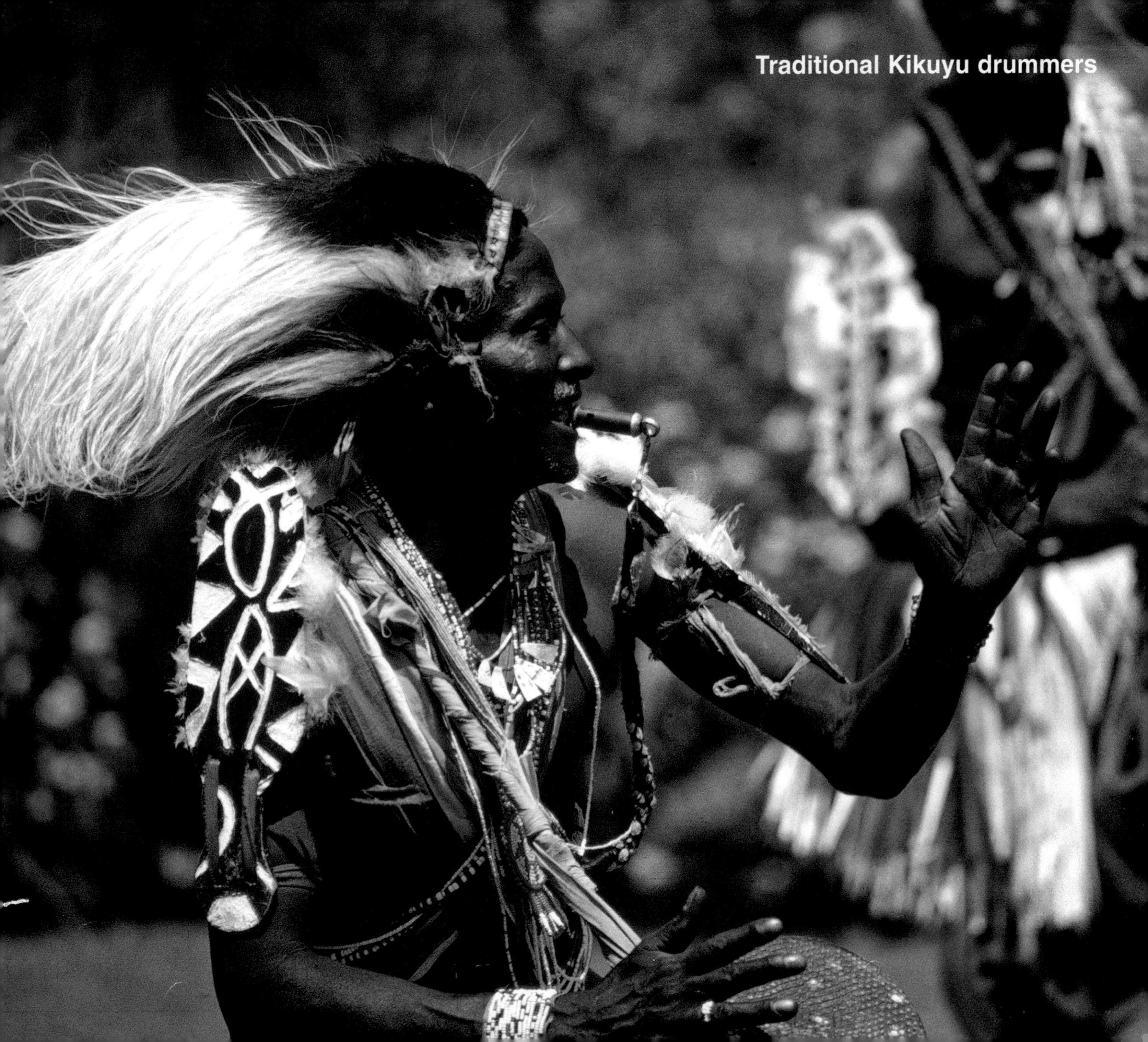
Traditional Kikuyu drummers

The capital city of Nairobi

City Life and Country Life

A Masai girl spreads mud and cow dung on her family's hut to help protect it from the rain.

Most of Kenya's people live in the country. But Kenya also has a few large cities. In the city, people live in houses or apartment buildings made from stone or concrete. Instead of tar or wood, the roofs of Kenyan houses are often shiny pieces of metal.

Life in the country is not the same in all areas. Some people live in huts with dirt floors and roofs made of mud, cow dung, and branches. Others travel all of the time. These people are usually young men who herd animals that feed on the grasslands. When the animals move along to find more food and water, the herders travel with them.

17

Schools and Language

When they are about six years old, Kenyan children begin school. Each morning before class, the students help get their classroom ready. They sweep and clean and straighten the desks. Then they sit down to begin class. They learn such things as history, math, science, and geography.

A Kenyan children's book in Swahili

The official languages of Kenya are English and Swahili (swah-HEE-lee). Swahili is a mixture of African and Arabic words. It is thousands of years old. Various ethnic groups speak many other languages. These languages are very different and very beautiful.

18

Students in Nairobi work together on their schoolwork.

Pickers in Kenya empty buckets of coffee beans.

Work

Farming is an important job in Kenya. Some Kenyans raise animals such as cattle. Others grow fruits and vegetables. Kenyan farmers also produce coffee, tea, sugarcane, cotton, and grains.

Another important job in Kenya is tourism. In this job, Kenyans show visitors from other places about their country. They lead safaris. They show visitors Kenya's many wild animals and tell them about the local people. Every year, more than one million people come to see and learn about Kenya.

A Masai man leads a tourist on a walking safari.

Food

Kenyans love white corn called maize (MAYZ). They crush it into a light flour and then cook all sorts of dishes with it.

One favorite dish is called *ugali* (oo-GAH-lee). It is made from maize and water. After it is cooked, it is thick and mushy. Kenyans pinch off a cooled piece and mold it into shapes to eat it.

Carrying corn in Kenya

Kenyans also eat fish, meat, and vegetables. And in big cities such as Nairobi, Kenyans find pizza and French fries to eat.

Young Kenyans with a homemade soccer ball

Pastimes

Just like in many other countries in the world, soccer is the favorite sport in Kenya. People play soccer everywhere!

Kenyans are also excellent runners. In fact, Kenyans have won dozens of Olympic medals for running events, including marathons.

Young Kenyans also like to make their own toys. Some children make cars or skateboards to play with. Others make dolls or balls. Children love to imagine things and often play hiding or hunting games.

Did you know?

Kenyan Paul Tergat (above) holds the marathon world record of 2 hours, 4 minutes, and 55 seconds. He set that record in 2003 in Berlin, Germany.

Holidays

With all of the different groups of people in Kenya, someone is always having a party. Some of the festivals are local celebrations. They are usually full of bright colors, music, singing, and dancing. Other holidays celebrate the whole country of Kenya. These days are packed with food and public speeches. Kenyans celebrate their Independence Day on December 12.

Kenya is a country that has worked hard for peace. Even though its people are diverse, Kenyans work together to make their country strong and proud. By respecting each other, Kenyans are showing other countries that fighting does not always solve problems.

Children perform at an Independence Day celebration in Nairobi.

Fast Facts About Kenya

Area: 225,000 square miles (582,650 square kilometers)—a little more than twice the size of Nevada

Population: About 34 million people

Capital City: Nairobi

Other Important Cities: Mombasa, Kisumu, Nakuru, and Eldoret

Money: The Kenyan shilling

National Language: English and Swahili are the official languages. There are also numerous local languages.

National Holiday: Independence Day, December 12 (1963)

Head of Government: The president of Kenya

Head of State: The president of Kenya

National Flag: Black, red, green, and white stripes. Two spears and a shield are shown in the middle of the flag. They stand for Kenya's will to defend its freedom.

Famous People:

Jomo Kenyatta: first president of Kenya, from 1964 to 1978

Mwai Kibaki: third president of Kenya

Louis and Richard Leakey: anthropologists (father and son)

Wangari Maathai: winner of the Nobel Peace Prize in 2004

Daniel arap Moi: president of Kenya from 1978 to 2002

James Ngugi wa Thiong'o: writer

Yvonne Adhiambo Owuor: writer

Paul Tergat: Olympic marathon runner

28

National Song: "Oh God of All Creation" (or "*Ee Mungu Nguvu Yetu*").
It was made the national song in 1963.

Oh God of all creation,
Bless this our land and nation.
Justice be our shield and defender,
May we dwell in unity,
Peace and liberty.
Plenty be found within our borders.

Let one and all arise
With hearts both strong and true.
Service be our earnest endeavor,
And our Homeland of Kenya,
Heritage of splendor,
Firm may we stand to defend.

Let all with one accord
In common bond united,
Build this our nation together,
And the glory of Kenya,
The fruit of our labor
Fill every heart with thanksgiving.

Kenyan Folktale:

How the Ostrich Got Its Long Neck

A short-necked ostrich isn't able to touch
the ground with its beak. The poor ostrich
has to sit to catch insects and can never reach the berries on the bushes.
A crocodile has a terrible toothache. The kind ostrich sticks its head into
the crocodile's mouth to take out the aching tooth. But then the crocodile's
jaws shut tight! There is a tug-of-war that leaves the ostrich with a stretchy
neck and newfound caution.

29

How Do You Say...

ENGLISH	SWAHILI	HOW TO SAY IT
hello	jambo	JAHM-boh
good-bye	kwaheri	kwah-HAY-ree
please	tafadhali	tah-fah-DAH-lee
thank you	asante	ah-SAHN-tay
one	moja	MOH-jah
two	mbili	MBEE-lee
three	tatu	TAH-too
Kenya	Kenya	KEEN-yah

Glossary

equator (i-KWAY-tur) The equator is an imaginary line around the middle of the earth. The equator divides Kenya almost in half.

ethnic groups (ETH-nik GROOPS) Ethnic groups are groups of people who share a way of life, language, or race. Kenya is home to many different ethnic groups.

immigrants (IH-mih-grents) Immigrants are newcomers from other countries. Years ago, many immigrants came to Kenya looking for good farmland.

reserves (ri-ZURVS) Reserves are places where animals can live safely. Kenya has many national parks and wildlife reserves.

safari (suh-FAH-ree) A safari is a trip on the savanna to see wild animals. Many people travel to Kenya to go on safaris.

savannas (suh-VA-nuhz) Savannas are huge grasslands. Many animals and birds live on Kenya's savannas.

Further Information

Read It

Aardema, Verna. *How the Ostrich Got Its Long Neck: A Tale from the Akamba of Kenya.* New York: Scholastic, 1995.

Bowden, Rob. *Kenya.* Chicago: Raintree, 2006.

Fontes, Justine and Ron. *Kenya.* Danbury, CT: Children's Press, 2001.

Giles, Bridget. *National Geographic Countries of the World: Kenya.* New York: National Geographic Children's Books, 2006.

Look It Up

Visit our Web page for lots of links about Kenya:
http://www.childsworld.com/links

Note to Parents, Teachers, and Librarians: We routinely verify our Web links to make sure they are safe, active sites—so encourage your readers to check them out!

Index